EROSION'S PULL

EROSION'S PULL

POEMS

Maureen Owen

COFFEE HOUSE PRESS

2006

Coffee House Press books are available to the trade through our primary distributor, Consortium Book Sales & Distribution, 1045 Westgate Drive, Saint Paul, MN 55114. For personal orders, catalogs, or other information, write to: Coffee House Press, 27 North Fourth Street, Suite 400, Minneapolis, MN 55401.

Coffee House Press is a nonprofit literary publishing house. Support from private foundations, corporate giving programs, government programs, and generous individuals help make the publication of our books possible. We gratefully acknowledge their support in detail in the back of this book.

Good books are brewing at coffeehousepress.org

LIBRARY OF CONGRESS CATALOGING-IN-PUBLICATION DATA
Owen, Maureen, 1943–
Erosion's pull / Maureen Owen.
p. cm.
ISBN-13: 978-1-56689-184-4 (alk. paper)
ISBN-10: 1-56689-184-1 (alk. paper)
I. Title.
PS3565.W558E76 2006
811'.54—DC22
2005035801

FIRST EDITION | FIRST PRINTING
1 3 5 7 9 8 6 4 2
Printed in the United States

ACKNOWLEDGMENTS

Some of these works have appeared in *Hanging Loose, Downtown, Inflatable, Tsunami, Barrow Street, Five Fingers Review, $lavery: Cyberzine of the Arts, Mark(s), 6ix, Chelsea, Long News: In the Short Century, The World, Columbia Poetry Review, Drawing Center Anthology, Courier, The Brink: Postmodern Poetry 1965 to Present, LIT, Titanic Operas, An Anthology of Guilford Poets,* and *The Call.*

With ongoing thanks to the Foundation for Contemporary Arts whose generous support made many of the works in this manuscript possible.

for Etta Place

Contents

Erosion's Pull

The recognition of the many types of feedback in the mountain-building system reveals that erosion not only participates in shaping mountains but also guides tectonic processes deep within the crust. The ultimate limiting force to mountain growth is gravity. Thus, erosion, by reducing the weight of the mountain range, actually accelerates tectonic processes beneath the mountains. For this reason, erosional processes can be viewed as "sucking" crust into mountain ranges and up toward the surface. And in this manner, erosion leaves a distinct fingerprint on the rocks and on the pattern of crustal deformation in and under mountains.

—*Scientific American*, April 1997,
 "How Erosion Builds Mountains,"
 Nicholas Pinter and Mark T. Brandon, p. 78

EROSION'S PULL

Whenever I snow

I think of Black
Beauty
when he was
pulling a cab

standing
streetside
under a lamppost
his dark harness gathering flakes
a jet horse becoming white   powder

a dark horse
disappearing

Goodbye to the Twentieth Century

or

Adios, Busy Signal

O Century   standing in the line of fire   A lake
on the slope of a plate   danger in the silverware drawer   O chaos
of looming disaster   where there are pots & pans teetering
no heart in the ketchup   no second-guessing the mustard

O little beep beep beep   O   So   long
nothing about you means anything anymore   only lost opportunities
O hello automated answering systems of the future   call waiting   O
voice mail   O pay phone at the frantic airport relaying delayed messages
"We're busy signal free," he said.   banishing forever   the busy signal

Traditionally   we were either there   or   we weren't
Now we can begin at the window   in a puddle of midnight
or sway in buckling air   a symbol of currency   and   decor
puffs rise out of the sugar bowl   Salt Spews

For most people the truly upsetting thing seemed to be
that Marilyn Monroe was home alone   on a Saturday night
O she who was found dead   nude   in bed with a telephone
the lyrical hiccup of the busy signal   tunneling her through the dark

I fell in love
I did it by myself

there are   some things you shouldn't do alone

her   hat blew off
it   happened   a   long time ago when you were small

Your arms describing angles on the   black sheets   at
each side of your head   guardians of abstraction   my
love has 2 minds   is   of 2 minds   two   I
thought I saw your two minds then   your two minds   both
of them in two heads   going in different directions
entirely &   I thought   here's what   I thought   What if
we were walking and we   thought   about something   that
might   have been going to happen   but didn't   we
thought it would have happened if we   hadn't been   there
thinking about it   & we wanted   to go back to a former
time   & not interfere   but the woman   on the news just
said that   "Many homeless people don't have furniture! . . . "
&   you are on your way out   into a rouge pigment spread
haphazard   on chunks of blue air   Nothing! say the
stars frozen into chips   nothing says their dark blanket
& soon you will be driving   through   Edward Hopper's
Cape Cod Evening   where only the dog looks happy

Now   even the jungle wanted him dead   or
she   closed   the   door behind her

Cuphea Platycentra

            "Cigar Flower"

        Mexico

charming little plant for the windowsill
scarlet tubular calyx

Ladies your little cigars aglow
where the eyes should be

plants   took the rest of the balcony

recording almost with complete detachment
the essential and transient nature of people & places
even this simple clapboard house
changes clothes

imagine a person or something heavy
pleated   forced to lean dangerously forward
Perhaps she has gone to her head

when we go away from everything
just like that   & mention

radiant energy from the
sun   crashing into the earth's atmosphere

to be so far from suffering   every step
a purpose   every day part of a divine plan
she hadn't seen it coming
putting the final coat on her resurrected luck!

Solving the slouch of the ruins!
the currents of the land   &
the ordinary immense to reflect
Seeing the batteries of milk!
the tambourines of the lights   She just
drove and drove

A History of the English Speaking Peoples   or

tea in the shape of a kite

the moon was scraping across the sky
what about the river   recognizable psyches should
have floated barely under the surface
water   in a bizarre reflection of leaky foliage

suspicious of their hands   they
held each other's noses   &
spun   the colors didn't move or slip out of joint
leaves were everywhere

When the eldest daughter   lost control of
the diesel tractor with the front loader   &
came through the wall of the dark living room   they
said hmmmmm   & put in a big picture window

Along this stream they demand more than a passing notice
Southward and eastward   along a terror
they who entered on a winter night   vanished
into deforested shapes

When the runaway pickup   with their 3 year old at
the wheel   took out one   of the two hefty columns
holding up the porch   they shook in the impact

not knowing what to look for   light   sheer as
white heat   large bundles of
straw   creamcolored & cut straight   &
added a sun deck

a spreading ink stain followed their sunsets
they were bigger than their chairs

Medusa's Hairdo

People point in different directions   They
are the opposite of information   a knuckle that
keeps growing   as everyone speaks of cats
I love only classic coke in the can
& read to myself about whales
dressed as Leonardo da Vinci explaining a working
model of his "heliocopter"
three days later the guy on the beach
is still there   unchanged
Or it would be like thinking I should never have had
that piece of pecan pie   the waitress hated me

between them & the birthday cake   a can of worms
on the table   as a painting of itself
each with another notion of what was going on
O Apostle of the Dark Ages   Go
ponder Grief!   Let the facts call up the imagination
let invention concur with inventions dream
rubber trees aren't made of rubber
sugar maples don't taste sweet
the prequel   before a sequel
determining the transparency of screen
the only way to use gravity as your source of movement
is to relax completely   & none of them
could agree on a single description of the horse

What a relief to see yourself suddenly again
after so many months like years of acres of
lumpy gravel   "Let me see that little face I love so well!"
But it was the fate of the other people that concerned
us really
they were all out there somewhere   watching fireworks
pointing
in different
directions.

Now This Vague Melancholy

Now this vague melancholy adores   me
of hours spent in your facade
it's best described as she can
if she could   likewise bitterly
since the forecast dented
with   our diner window cut in two
    , as if her life

her life dissolving
in what had been agreed
not to tell to one another
what was   is the danger
the story of the stories
And   this melancholy.

if then we couldn't stretch the seams
of our need   while being chatty
we could discuss

                              long into noted
all else
sweet melancholy   dished
each by itself   into a darker   ness
where the hangover begins before midnight
& I could talk to you forever
for no good reasons science could explain
for we are two of repelling cogs
set in their motion fast by some diligent

terrain rising flat as the prairie
as a word   I fell in love with you   then
with a word   can such a thing be done
because of a word   you said   Nebraska
& all the chairs drew back their doors
& all the floors burst into flame
& in the night a single fire swept
swept through it all   &   I woke kneeling on
charred ground   & it was as the saint

proclaimed

They can't handle the day shift   or
                    vespertinal jockeys

she was thinking   "I could just spit"
I could get falling down substance abused
I could burn myself with a cigarette   I
could smoke   a cigarette   I could disguise myself
as mayhem   I could turn on the dancers   I
could stomp out the bluffs where they press
their lips together   & stare at the fat moon from
their snotty embrace   O half-baked idea!
rising a thousand years out of chalk dust   &
pleated yellow light   I could search for the
same weather   compare time to Paradise
a face in a window   patient & eager
as the beloved appears   to hit the road
temperature & the economy   the walls of state

but you could look all day &
not find a weasel in the desert

must love constantly remind love that it is
love   for the many we are not   Shout
in a parking lot   they are the same people
dodging a dark glance from an exlover's eyes
the visual spectrum arches
stars gather under their sleeping bodies   mattresses
wonder what they were really meant to be

Sometimes it's not who you're with
but what happens to you when you're with them
Petals from the pear tree blossoms whirled around
her head   humidors flew open
she had been living in someone else's house
on someone else's avenue
in someone else's relationship
for someone else's dream
& now
she was leaving

I'm not alone
When I'm on the phone.

the trampling of the Prince   was in all the papers
to wait singed hours in the wideness outside a window
he comes and stands in the crocuses
    priceless tapestry gathers on his thigh
    he is trying to pick out a castle
& so the secret pewter debacle   the handsome garage
the flamboyant pump   the sultry beauty of the woodpile
the gorgeous stumpage and knobby-kneed lumps of moss
the clothesline a litany   in Latin

so shadow of a shadow seen running
tumbling forward   giddy of dreadful swooning
wrongful capacity   he said he had to turn the jar
inside out   to get at it   arresting it was nature
to have come this far   ours is only the space between
the paint   & when it sings it sings like the logic of gasping
it cajoles   our urge to hear

Big shoes abandoned in boredom   have leveled the Prince!
the media   all of its strangers   goes home
now flawlessly they straddle the walls of the estate
like holiness the singed hours fall
there is no answer they know how to wait for
they always come here

out of the little curtain of disenchantment the wandering bagel rolled

and over the toes of the establishment it rolled and across the boulevard

of despair and into the city of water where fountains lashed into the sky

and turned wildly their great liquid eyes so that the fair dreams shimmering in the afternoon heat

rose slowly to their feet and took a determined stroll about the plaza past the expatriate intently

reading the newspapers from home with gripping fingers and thoughts of what it was to be a

citizen—a citizen!—responsible and debonair to whom the men came   for advice   and to

whom the women came   for advice

#6

I was skiing along the edge of the soccer field   looking
all legs   when I saw a neighbor   straight out of an
Ingmar Bergman film skiing toward me   As we passed in a stark
moment of wind-whipped snow I said   referring to my nascent
status on skis   "I'm just learning"   —   "We all are" he said with
a nod   and glided on

Plaudit

or   she found herself mesmerized by the hand gestures of the mourners

I did not the ultimate concern of ever myself   but
I am the evidence
considered   the classic theme just set that right over here
under the fig tree   where I imagine the garden would be   & gather
up those precious thoughts of indigo and stealth   the thieves didn't
think we were rich enough to mug   but see we did something!   some of this stuff is ours

Chrome & glass doors swing open
Jane   with the sun behind her
                    Snow stockings
last night I dreamed I was a Buddhist
You were always coming and going   and going   and going

until
       you just left   over   and over   and over
until finally you were just leftovers   leftover from that
big dinner   party   we invited so many people to
I couldn't find you to ask where   did you put the cold beers   I
COULDN'T FIND YOU AT ALL   WERE YOU THERE ANYWHERE
or had you left already driving down the coast with your first girlfriend's daughter

a portable pinup spray painted on the process
                    sparkling like coins   or

            the condition of a crowd adjourning the opera

                        Ave Maria   Ave maria   ave Maria

Portraiture

or I tripped on a crown of thorns   crossing the yard   or
everything goes into the big stew   that is you

O Saint
Cecilia   stripped with wounds
ribbons of green & sea green   all gilt's golden
chipped & peeling   taffeta shroud
O Saint Cecilia!   How
diversified
how diversified is
your portfolio

O Saint Cecile
soft folds to cushion the bridge of your nose
quietly broken   your ivory skin   raked in a pattern
tucked in a virtue saint of dropped futures   Basilicae
right in Toulouse-Lautrec's hometown!
left to perfection now   a
scarf of blood to wrap your hair

                                        orange
to cradle your face   forehead   all quietly broken
your cream painted skin

O Cecilia
what violence left a sleeper so   dreaming in plaster
stretched in   mute pigment
window still as a glaze   of
itself   Patron saint of leaves hammered into a steel grey sky!

enameled martyr

O   Saint Cecilia! who will not be back   onlyin this
sensuous paste
how diversified
how diversified is

your portfolio

fare ye well   fare ye well
I love you more   than words can tell
                    —The Grateful Dead

flaxstraw broom   on a long handle   or

                              perles Among hogges

a woman stands waist deep in water   a woman stands
in waist deep water   She is sweeping
the bottom   of the lake

these hollow glass beads   colored by the pearly dust which falls from the scales of
the little fish known as   the bleak   when repeatedly agitated in water
real clothes and   I thought he said   they were arrested for stealing   a wave
twilight began to erase the yards   full of objects   one
at a time   I heard him say   they were jailed for stealing
a wave   he had no clothes on the top half of his body   the world slowly
shading   her vigil   owning no furniture he hung his walls   with pictures
of the furniture he would have if he could afford to buy it   & a newscaster just described a
would-be bank robber as   pretending his gun was a hand!   then hastily corrected himself.
Imitation Pearls!   they were   imitation pearls   not the real thing
maybe to be here   it is necessary to go there   to be somewhere else   in order to be
where you are   my manner there would be my manner here   but I would see myself
from an outsider's point of view   All my demons   previous   My desperation lost   & wan-
dering [agoraphobically] without me   My desires corrugating   like the uncle who dove
from his ship into a freezing sea in Fellini's movie *Americord*   & began screaming "My nuts are
shriveled up like a peanut!"   O then to reverse my ignorance   to make the other
into the allure—I know what I do not know—affords me   crumpled linen

Imitation Pearls   before swine!

                                 Casting Imitation Pearls before swine!

but to the swine they appeared   to be

                                Valueless   just like   real pearls

darkness sprang the swans   from the shellacked pond

or
blue
cerulean
a kind of plum   blue gum
veins through skin
steel at twilight   thin milk
vapor   over a soggy ground

breasts in motion in Matisse's   *Goldfish and Sculpture*

from outside the sun has chewed through the stucco and laths
& now   waits at the far end of the room   a gold bar   of light
mixed into a flat paint   where somehow leaves are withdrawing

up a flesh-colored widening funnel   tho
the misanthropic orange fish   in the green glass cylinder
don't give a hoot   what you say to me in my dreams   Matisse
has stuck some flowers in a fancy vase   and painted a short green shelf
I haven't mentioned   with what seems to be a tiny glazed window
above it   & shoveled all   model flowers fish foliage heat   &
into a heap   in the center of the canvas   brushing azure everywhere   else   in a
flurry over walls table & floor   to cool off!   the moment   the
passion of objects   the scorching afternoon outside   impasto! no!

How calm the cafés have become now!
the smallest margins of the seams glow   through   an eerie iridescence palms

a man follows a woman with a jar on her

head   through the stalls in a foreign city   that same day
a sand painting is destroyed on the boulevard   coming out of
their skin and hair on fire   the shape of the limbs   into the crowd

come together   in an argument of form

        a real outlaw is   much better without the tie

like the broken asphalt of a deserted school yard
the flowers are a pool of blue water   under my skin

 you've gotten   under my skin

A "Mad" but Compelling Vision

> or he's in the castle   but focused out

now   take the word   passion
do you carry it with you through the darkness
will it describe your arrival at a place I cannot
I cannot imagine you passionate
I cannot close the car door or latch whatever
Is what sits behind your going less than passion
or is it more   An undertow of speechlessness filling
all the spaces you travel out of   drawn forward
or is it merely in the direction you are facing
you are going

I can't imagine what is keeping me up   or

                                        a slab of   vision

girl with a jar on her head
fellow with a stuffed bird on his
tourists who began arriving   couldn't resist
asking to buy a water jug right off   a woman's head

ebony nightcloth lifted sideways   bends a destination
fragrant   curls hanging over a keyboard   a truncated portraiture   often
funerary in purpose   what future planned with teacup and logger boots
that time we were dying   we had figured out how   our time was short
now the cut had almost totally healed   since the day before the day
she had slipped   the newly sharpened blade out of the pie   &
across her underknuckle

Reality is the last word in illusionism   when the lifelike figure stretches
its limbs   and rises   the amazing magical trick is over   it is simply
a real person

it was that color that night is   when you can't see anything   dark
carved out in 3-dimensional form   a stone object   blockish
black stacked up   where he had returned   & left again
the sand painter had deliberately changed the designs   so that
the painting was no longer sacred.   and the order of the streets
covering now   any trace of him

nobility is the furthest from here   he will take a walk in the park
I think I shall become formidable   I shall sentence all who have betrayed me
shall they be   allowed   to defend their extraordinary degrees of illusion

27

to   Madonnas and saints   roses pressed against their chests
every mole & flaw   every pronoun   stripped down to resemble its foe
We will understand the purpose of clothing then   and how it came
to take the place of skin   tattoos under layers of fabric   scars submerged
plunged under   her headdress

Nox

or   the boys are rightly pale

                                                                or A study   in snow

What
Wide black absences of snow   where the trees block the light

crisp prongs and tripods
tall black shadows   of the
thick trunks and spindly branches line up on glossy flounces

Sargent's *Two Girls in White Dresses*   arrive
in their mob of linen and gossamer

Earlier that same night
the stone wall has snow in its teeth
a white rash shrugs over the gravel drive
    the used car dealer lugs the huge mechanical monkey
back inside

at night a table set with shadows   colossal
where yard billows up   dark stripes   out of heavy white taffeta
slapping knees & thighs   sheer   fluted
through   A twelve-paned dark-tinted glass box

hijacked space   that's not the way you'd
wanted him to go   he wanted to go home   to stay at home in the first place.
he wanted to be a girl in a corporate garden café soup kitchen waterfall
to the right of the road for miles the sea went on a blue beverage   complete with ice

after working for weeks   she realized late one night   she
had already written the piece   some years before
She covered the bank's pillars with puffy large circular plastic molds
with bagel look-alikes   Studied
and studied   only to realize   that everyone knew already
what she was about   to discover

he was the one among us   whose name began with a vowel

I don't suppose the nieces could ever be more serious than they were tonight

Pope Paul has cleared the way   for   dozens
of martyrs to become saints   what can you say about a situation like
that   today   people I hadn't seen   in any permanent manner
backed up to go the wrong way to talk to me

&Don't the feathered kachina dance   between

the boy says   he didn't mean to do it   &wants to know   when
you photographed Astor Place in 1947   &   I was sorting wet stones
he can carry red tulips again   the mother says her son needs counseling   &she's
trying to regain custody   from an aunt
 in that deep puddle in the gravel drive   the one that held my favorites
soaked to a high gloss
&where's the dad besides being in lilacs   his lawyer says he's contacted   at
least 20 companies   about a book   a movie deal
the railroad track looks like stitches from the hybrid roses of the air

&Who is this famous redhead?   Woodpecker   doll of the underworld

O! When you shot Astor Place in 1947 with your best lens
& none of those being photographed knew   this was how they would look

&if I am in the walking   I will cross unto the triangle   where the subway waits for me
already the token is annoying

"and watched the sun come rising
from that little Minnesota town."
—Dylan

The Wounded Day

To all appearances they came   hats& coats
left smoldering in the rain under the skin   that map of
land we'd traverse eventually   & left to our own devices   We
would tunnel into the brain of June bugs
& disclose all that we found

in California my mother said

     start someplace where you are figuring it out
wait for a clarity to form in the dusk & turquoise light
the world's first moth-eaten plan   will solve all your problems
right from the start   which you can't go back to by the way   but you can
because you grow   because you grow up   You can no longer
you can no longer   you can no longer   reply

for Hannah Weiner

Secrets of the Cover Girl

       or   **the Fair & square silk ribbon in the middle of the road**

I can swim but I can't fly

puce aurora borealis
lake in a storm blue or gun metal grey
sunset lemon
raspberry & billowed us
brushing horses
ochre or salmon spread thin
the little mirror beside my grandmother's bed

the woman got up to fix the projector
the family bunny   the family pony the family washcloth

now the dark sizzles with insect life
sulfurous yellow moon in the black leaves

on theory   take a bit that interests you   and chew
But don't just stand there
how stunning you are,
Nature   in yr gorgeous hypnotic violence

one doesn't simply live in the world   one must continually read it
in cutout letters

on the faces of friends
Audrey Hepburn wore a size 10 shoe all her adult life
the glistening instep   a white-glazed terra-cotta
"Sheffield Pure Milk"   bottling plant

and Hannah Weiner won't ever tap me on the shoulder at the Ear Inn again

"... that the burden of unavoidable unhappiness is increased by unhappiness about being unhappy."
—Edith Weisskopf-Joelson

for Dora Maar

Picasso's Chair

or   Breaking out   in thorns

she is weeping
doing dishes like the storm

he stays away from the house   his torso is up in arms

their language has become gibberish   she calls nightly
asking the same question   a car door slams

the lawnmower flies through the violets   scattering chipped buttercups
into enameled air

such a state   such a state to be in   she snaps
the door behind her
he paints for hours   then does sit-ups
          she doesn't come back   that night   or the next
doesn't return to pose for *Weeping Woman   Woman Reclining with a Book* or *Woman
Combing Her Hair*   doesn't photograph *Guernica*'s various stages while he paints.
without her record   he finds it less interesting to continue
gradually he abandons the painting   *Guernica* in the corner   unfinished

dazed by her own perfumes   the moon
is in the dark

he has come down the stairs   he has faced   a similar being
he has collapsed onto the molding   modeling his own jacket   as
a blanket

when they set up his studio   under the perfect flat stone a flock of ants
was sleeping
she knew all the cooks   all the chefs knew her name
now he's gone   Spanish Johnny   on his back with her hand over her mouth
only walking   her ship of leg & limb   her body   large bare feet on the street outside
what gets wet is hair or hats   umbrellas   sleeve   & lilac all leak of rain gear spots

No Salt! No Salt!   the stars cry out   she cannot see the sea that's drops of water
We bury what we should have said   in gravel   in pitch   In sand
he'd really rather leave it open   a certain amount of ambivalence
about giving up his independence
He is said to have remarked he could never   see her
never imagine her   except crying
the alphabet and the day go down in the grass
pink   horses   flush
the scenery   takes care of itself
she sees how it is   whether or not she saw other people
    Who really needs this guy!

he placed the glass of wine in front of her   she thanked him only to
hear him say "that's not for you" "you can have some, but that's mine"
she had gained too much weight since the wedding
his gesture not a gesture but only the inexact outline of one

she lit a cigarette   it was for her the need to set something on fire
the venetian blinds gave them prison uniforms

But where were the long sultry nights of the Kalahari
the campfires of the caravans
breezes whipped up from   the bazaars of Zaire

                    Where   were the Zebras!

A Moroccan Sun Visits Connecticut

Stacks of window sash   emu= bird
lying in bed   buttered
on wcbs this morning robert stack is saying
"If only
      your home was alarmed"

editing landscapes

or the experience was different than   the experience

in my fever
he walked in a field of huge upturned milk cartons
& had brought along 12 suitcases
it was still daylight
it was still just light enough to see that it
had begun to snow
several cars were in the parking lot   the scenery
was becoming more demanding   mercurial
him in the amethyst leaves   stained
damp umber   fresh wet sotted greens and darker red
there was a tower
citizens came flying   out of it
repeatedly blown sideways   then hurling straight
downward   appearing when you'd least expect it
they'd get up   brush themselves off
rubbing their cuts & bruises
          only to lurch back up the uneven stone steps

they could be heard chanting
                    "a tooth is coming loose"
                    "a tooth is coming loose"

& seemed obsessed   like the twirling dog
on the David Letterman Show   or convinced
of a constant absence   of other   possibilities

it was the summer I was pretty much involved with   thinking
about being involved with someone   who was involved   with
someone else   What
I wasn't   Where
I wasn't   What
education I didn't have   wearing
a black & white checkered shirt
precise squares   loose but gathered at
strategic moments   He
wore a brass buttoned navy blazer,   &
seemed to have polished his face
  the glare bouncing off his complexion became enormous
  neither could see where the other was going   We
began to experience an industrial anxiety   With him
I felt it was wrong   to say something was wrong
there was this person   he walked on his feet   to
this shoreless beach   waveless
waterless beach   to this beach without a shore
Burning burning burning burning

O over every life-sized drought

          or   a solid interval between crenels on a battlemented parapet

              or   just say "no"

I can't help you
I didn't get up this morning
I didn't pay my taxes on time
I didn't return the damn video to the damn video store pick you up at the train station rescue the
sailors trapped in the sunken sub
you can't count on me
I won't be there for you   I'm not
myself   I won't drop in just to say Hi   When you
need a friend   forget it   don't look over here   a shoulder to cry
on   that won't be me, toots   through thick & thin   Don't
hold your breath   It isn't me on that ringing phone   Do you have a problem?
I won't be solving it

**the Leaving Song   or   where would we be if we
weren't   where we are**

he didn't want to say to me what they had said to him
causing him to say to me   he didn't feel
like going into it right now   Somewhere out in Chicago darkness
a couple of eyes floated through urban neighborhoods &

What made it so different   so it couldn't just sit still
so it couldn't fold into itself and be what it was
was this desire this ripping intensity this standard moment
the trivial present the second that is the flash in the pan
lull before the storm, chance of a lifetime
wave to catch   last bus outa town   right place at the

in the moment of the story she was writing without words
their glances parted the air   struggling   constructing a
dam   how would it work now   a relationship shifted altered
permanently forever after the sound his voice refused to make

She sat in the humid dark   with the man who was getting to know
himself   jungle cries between the spaces   in the trees

          (If she had sent the tulips   if she had not
          worn the shirt   if she had ordered the wood
          fixed the stovepipe graduated from college   changed
          the tires on her jeep   used the ice cream maker
          he gave her for Christmas learned how to swim the
          American Crawl the butterfly stroke the dive if she

had drank more or less   if she had been constant and
always understanding   if she had agreed more   let
him run the show   plan their days   if his girlfriend
could have gone on living with them   if he   had been
a god   or brilliant and if she had stuck by him until
proven as such   if she had taken photos   famous photos of him in all
stages of his life   if she had documented his days   applauded
his work   if she had seen the axle come apart or noticed
the sound of the tire   Before it went flat   if she had not
laughed at the small   electrical smoke plume rising from
the dashboard of his brother's
car   O I
                         suppose things   would have gone differently

that morning   in the rearview mirror   a pastoral 18th-century painting
the light of day fanning   through the branches)

at the gathering   a woman took hold of the mask and pulled
it off the face of the morose intruder   who was   her cousin
playing a joke on her.   Those horrible two last lines she shrieked
she was thinking   of the sonnet   & of the tall cartoonist dressed
in black leather with a long tattoo
on her forearm   a pair of rolling skulls   She would tell us she
had left the circus for good
clumsy white camels   growling & coughing
Graceful as swaying moonlight   or florescent paste
Why not spend my time living in a movie full
of blue tables? she thought   on the morning news an 86-year-old
woman receives an 8-million-dollar phone bill   What
is the shape of the dream   when you wake up into it   Can
we imagine the stick figure   of a rotund Anglican   Or

how a simple love of geometry   can   cause you to stay in the same place
too long

        After the adoption
           of the anti-Jewish laws in France
        tho he hadn't wanted to leave   Chagall
        began to realize he must   but
        anxiously asking of Varian Fry
        "Are there cows in America?"

the gods are peeling off the temple walls
    or   **a guide is usually someone who's**   **done this before**

If the brisk   trade winds die down   Remember the guidebook warning   about sand flies

in the photo   the shadow of my nose has fallen
over my front tooth so it appears   missing

a male voice singing in Latin
as grain stubble

Rock stars   have so much money   they never have to
stand in line to get into the clubs   they
go right past people waiting in the cold for hours   Our
nerves are so unprofitable   but they   live in Emerson's undated calendar days
twice heavenly   they scramble through the rain into a limousine

Now   you take my picture on a bridge in Florence   the sun is shining   we
have come by train   we see more jewelry than we have ever seen in one place before
bracelets of leather & crystal & gold   Not the tombs of Ramses   But O Dante's
Memorial and Michelangelo's grave   I doubt   you don't   Where is the home we
left behind   & where are our pajamas
the red ones with the blue cowgirls twirling their lassos over their heads   as
they ride their buckskin at full gallop   they are you in the wild barebacked days
with your hair so long and black   you & your wild girlband on horseback
the selves of our own history
have forgiven each other

6 from the Joe Cornell Series

a group of girls from Minnesota

                    or   black mascara

Not trees trace so   just kids we   hung
slim buckets of chokecherries from our wrists

in neighboring galaxies   Giant Star Factories take control
composed of cold hydrogen gas and dust

7,000   light years from earth
slender-toed geckos   step onto the moon

On the road between 2 baptisms and a shower they rang
to say   shallow water   the mouths drop open

not where you stand but how long you can
stand standing there
in constant hypothesis

the trees are passersby
mercurial
damp light
flat orange moon
velvet navy-blue sky

fire berries
from here we see the beautifully attired drive tough Ford pickups

the oncoming
organizing principle
brushed out

the dancers take turns leaping over the bonfire   into
Qué pasa USA?

haircuts in London are really pretty backward
London—you are definitely not going to have a manicure there!
in L.A. toes must match the hands or else just don't leave the house
in N.Y. it's more brunette

Outside   a refrigerator   floats in the blackness   shiny amid sharp stars

& the turtle who holds up the world   holds up
the world

In the winter
> **we have sleeves**

but in the summer
> **we have arms**

I have become friends   with the man
who talks to himself
sometimes   we   wait for a train   or
disembark at the same station   folding   watching
the trees   languid   dense   rolling upward   then backing over themselves

The way Vanessa Bell painted portraits of *all* Clive Bell's mistresses   Slow
brushing the light   Nearby
Virginia Woolf reclines in a deck chair   reading   *Story Without a Name*—for Max Ernst. c. 1942
four sets of four   full of all size sounds
on the steps
of   Our Lady of Pompeii   Church
no one asks her to move!   not injured Christian soldier   nor injured Knight in a work shirt back
from the Holy Wars   the Crusades   claims the church for France   For local folk   For Little
Italy   for the sake of God   for God's sake!   for the hull of the ship was human
the way water & fire   look alike   do they?

past the pewter rims of my glasses

The inlets are beautiful
tonight,   the waters done   in subtle chalks and water paints
neon signs sizzle   in the dusk   By the time I arrived at Duncan Grant's
Still Life with Eggs 1930   I realized   I was quite hungry

for Susan B and Susan H

Soap Bubble Set. 1936

> or   **that's when she said**
>   **—Does it matter**
>   **which one**
>   **is which—**

Today Susan added the wings of butterflies   she found in the vegetable garden
near the cabbages   to her painting   rasping insect songs clamor in
the summer dark
their perfectly repetitious patterns repeat a single phrase   Over
& over   every night I've had to get out of bed to capture two moths
with a little green net (formerly used to catch tropical fish in a ten gallon tank)
& raise the screen to shake them outside   some nights I net them quickly
other times they beat their wings frantically & dart about So I can't corner them   I've
begun to wonder   Am I tossing the same 2 moths   up &Toward
Jupiter's Moon Io a world so volcanically hyperactive
that nearly its entire surface is likely to be lava still in various stages
of cooling
>   Both think
>   I've done too much for 3   while that one & another
>   feel I've a special   bond with the middle
>   naturally the digit in between & the most
>   recent are sure the first has
>   been getting far too much consideration

waiting for the audition Jennifer ran out of money   and slept in a park
Proving once again   Madonna don't care What we wear!

now   He has set the box astir
in its dark realm of edges & angles
what whispers will bubble upwards of
nickel & dime illumination   or lampshades of packed gauze

it's pitch outside   until I turn off the light
inside.
the moon is in the night sky   but the geography
of the moon   is on the chart   Today an easier way to do things
emerged   She had laid the white pages out   over tables
as though they were small steps   one leading to the next.

Hotel Ozean, 1959–1960   Samples
       of the blaze   or if she moved away would the magic mirror
                              still be magic in the   new location

In a desperate moment of outlaw crazy senseless aloneness realism   netting atoms
from the solar wind   the involutions
of his shirt flowing   & burning   this treasured smidgen of the Sun
the insects had stopped grinding corn
  In the yard
Beatrice addressing Dante from the car   mouthed "Unless you go to Cologne you're not
likely to see this."   red oval lips

framing   a gilt (yellow likegold)
A
large thin copper rings   one tossing   loops
blue elephant under a red railroad trestle of block
long white pipe with shipping labels plastered over the stem
not the hue of tofu   but desert regalia   Tantrum segments   Most people
are afraid to say extravagant things definitively   for instance
Key West is tired of chickens in the road
          sometimes passionate clucking
          sometimes
          a strangled squawk
cracked paint the color of twine   On the platform the conductor lifts his hat   sweeps
the sweat back through damp hair   96&humid   from the air-conditioned train I
watch him   I am searching   for a philosophy   a putty sky   cloudy   but not
too cloudy   & there are   you know   angels with trumpets

**not every restaurant that attracts celebrities
has an attitude**

               O Hotel Bon Port! (1954)   O Florence

See for yourself   how the small lichen is
the only garment on the boulder

It's hot, humid midday
a man & another
get into their car in
a dense circle of shade
under a small tree

we went to a terrible place
we tried all the restaurants
there wasn't a celebrity in the mob
tho the swimming pool was filled with lava

rock from the car stereos played along the river wall

"I have no dry ice!" complained the DJ
the onlookers seem as enraptured as they did
hours ago

What is the purpose of a dik-dik?

it often took the whole day to get 1 print right
manipulating the work tremendously in the darkroom
the idea of inner emptiness   was devastating then

being inside the construction's hot white blinding   scorched
itinerary   light nips at our heels   passports pinned to our underwear
           an odd detail of stamp-sized portraits

the word "kangaroo"   in the aboriginal language
simply means "I don't understand."

for Kyran

"*Every ship is a romantic object, except that we sail in.*"

                         —R.W. Emerson

My Little Sister's Mercedes

Winter time frost on the
crater wall   & dark sand
dunes on the floor

happy birthday   it's your birthday
you say the bay is full of white sails
on a blue sky

the scholars
are back in the tombs   or on the haunted
fields of Gettysburg

a woman waiting for the #6
on the subway platform   had a copy
tucked under her arm

moon at the power of 241 candles per foot
the students put their satellite in the
back of the pickup & drove
to the air force base for testing

Sunlight makes the backwater sluice
go cornflower
& the stiff rusty reeds of the marsh

then the dream spoke
she knew   it was   Life with   who
took no notice of her as a woman

showing up unbidden and unannounced
mute rains begin to pillow the deep snow
for instance, the fabric didn't come from a store

L'Egypte   circa 1940
12 corked pristine bottles
marbled end papers
tiny spoons

Suddenly   I realized I'd
forgotten that birds have hearts
yes little tiny hearts
in their little feathered chests

                               he didn't want to be even more alone

             or   Unplanted space

In *The Blue Dahlia*   William Bendix has
a metal plate in his head   & hears drummers drumming
but it's not the neighbors   it's the gulls dropping through fog
into the blurred violet of the tidal flats   the sea outside the harbor darker blue
& over the closer half-emptied estuary the thin lighter blues & shimmering pinks   sun
gone down   but lingering somehow over still water & little boats moored softly where in electric
Red on dull cornflower sky the Pitney Bowes sign near the gone dark
McCalls   windows shards of sky greyish salmon at horizon then smearing into bluer to a
denser more opaque as it rises   leaving houses of rectangular design &
streetlights' crepuscular give way to blotted night   as lighted panes allow   interior views
of rooms lamps tables staircases   woodish floors
train pulling in over water a bridge a port like station   like the railing on a ship   & it's all
about relationships   how a nervous person just wants to come home   Bendix sees
the shadow of the bar on the reflection of the light on the windowglass
is a tiger's eye
five of them
in odd array

Nearly Snowing

or
(now the wash of white
falls like a drape or curtain
a thin linen over the
small forest   at the edge   of the field)

or "We've had a rather
stormy autumn in space, which has been great for checking out our instruments."

the snow enters the grey and umber forest
from above
and so amid the trunks of trees that bear no resemblance to themselves as seen
in sleek and headdress

a mauve pale as hushed washes
snow in the grey and umber afternoon
thin white linen   flung
over trees at the edge of the field

sit   amid the grey and umber trunks
before the long journey
sit in the grey and mauve afternoon
the umber trunks

wash of mauve   pale as hushed choirs   fills the branches
dense white mist

a wash of white
falls like
thin linen over the
small edge   of the field

The ion and electron monitors were turned on several months ago in preparation for their role during solar-wind collection. The monitors communicate with Earth frequently and will give periodic solar-wind weather reports. "It has been exciting watching the space weather so far," said Dr. Roger Wiens of Los Alamos National Laboratory, NM, head of the team that operates the instruments. "We've had a rather stormy autumn in space, which has been great for checking out our instruments."

Clouds over Chicago

he said
I don't like to meet people I don't know

I don't like to meet people I don't know
                              he said

on the brow of
a little moss
where no one lives   **or**

           brushing horses

baffling

who sees the horse of bafflement   a color so desperate
who knows the tone of your extent
baffled
O inventor of the man of your dreams!
take off your glasses!   and let the scenery drip toward the sea
      where it will take care of itself

Humans are not the regular diet of bears
humans are not in a bear's diet
said the deep furred bear
to the woman   in the tree

a horde of pigeons were pecking around his feet
he did not say how long it would last

moon through lace   curtain
through lacy locust branches

moon in a circle of
locust limbs
all day I thought about   the different ways of telling a story
a particular story   one that was true   then the

       Milky Way

      sparkling like coins
           diamonds have gathered under the leaves

where the boy is temporarily
Don't try to solve the problem
         rather ponder the events
         snack food for the fishes
         small stones

now bored by everything she once held sacred O dear
becoming the solitary figure from behind   staring flat at sea
embedded wind and spray   and the whippet reeds of the marshes
Was bored the right word?   pursed lips
a language stuck in the mud   camera bashed on the barnacles   tiny
snails everywhere   tiny snails everywhere   tiny snails everywhere!
gulls screeching at them!   tide taking everything back

let it go away   the sway of wonderment   rolled   out like a carpet because   I ate

       all the money,

            honey

What Shape Rhapsody

tomorrow   apparently   it will
snow even more fiercely
the carriage house roof has collapsed   under the weight
winter is not over   I telephone
the furnace service for the third time
this week. After each repair the
fumes are worse than ever   at least
we have the wood burning stove   and wood to split
albeit it's dark   wet   tho all the piping in the pantry
will probably freeze anyway   we've had the hair dryer
on them every night   Why not
leave them dripping?   But the drains freeze up
& those upstairs present a flood to all our books below
pots & towels must be rushed in   Now even
the washing machine hums without moving

Yes   the invincible storm door has broken
water pipes both hot & cold are frozen everywhere
all of us have fallen at least once on the corona of silk
frozen sheen   gleaming & cruel   en route to jeep & pickup
the path to the barn between two dwarf glaciers
& the ice in   the pony's   bucket went
clear to the bottom   solid
and rolled out in the shape of a carved
hat   from a winter carnival
the air's
as cold as breaking glass   so dry at night
the crystals spark & sizzle   as if

the dark was full of fireflies   the
solitary cat   camps in the hayloft
this morning a stalk of green alfalfa
stuck out of his tail   plumish
&   oddly disturbing

Pinatubo

you're the new bow

in the sky

. . . certainty of being is concentrated, and we have the impression that . . .

deep deeper deep
the flagstone marsh
the flagstone marshes these
the deep
the do you
the do you want it to be true
do you want it to be true
do you want it to be true
do   you   do you want it to
be true   you do
you do something to me
you do something
to me   do you want it to be true
do you want it to be true
what do you want it to be
do you want   is it want
do you want
does want want you to want what is want any way
Anyway what is want anyway
want means you have to have it or
you die
too painful to live and not get
get what you want too
painful to live you die
and not get what you want
this is painful to want
I want you to want me
I want you to want me this
is what I want

and if I got what I wanted you would want me
you would want me   to want you
Then we could progress
we could
progress by wants' wants
small curved flagstones set in a
rural environment
smooth rounded wants that we can step
on as we walk up from the boathouse
having just climbed
slightly damp and springy
out of the rowing boat
the lovely wooden skiff
now moored   on the marsh

Fvsh'ot
Fash'on

Fashion

Behind the zombies
the dwarf vampire boy   wears large
white mittens   perfect cutouts
in red brick   his
droopy cape   absorbed into
walls of corrugated tin
fire escapes   shelved
above his peaked
head

the moon on the water

bounced into the trees

every limb

After Shōnagon

for ron padgett and george schneeman

Coming up First Ave this morning   I ran into Ron
& George on the corner of 10th street. They looked
magnificent as they came toward me. Their splendid,
cherry-colored Court cloaks were lined with material
of the most delightful hue and lustre. Ron wore dark
grape-colored trousers, boldly splashed with designs
of wisteria branches: his crimson under-robe was so
glossy that it seemed to sparkle, while underneath
one could make out layer upon layer of white and light
violet robes. The cherry-colored Court cloak George
was wearing was sufficiently worn to have lost its
stiffness, a white under-robe buffeted loose trousers
of dark purple. From beneath the cloak shone the
pattern of another robe of dark red damask. They had
just come from viewing the u no hana and were each
carrying nothing in their hands but a single spray of
the white blossoms.

for Glen Baxter

Perfect English

. . . just some peaceful gardens by the sea
buttercups lolling on a hill
stone fences   tumbled rocks & tea
sweet bees on doorjamb   & windowsill
& the lump   of a foot   by the gate . . .

The Wedding

    I

I was wearing my Bambi meets Godzilla t-shirt
a wall of family faces   relatives' eyes
were staring out   between the blooming chrysanthemums

    II

"spacey" space, he said
"people think you're spacey"   full
  of space I thought   like grace

Small Parts

blue scilla flood the slope behind the house
it's red   a fever in the small grey rain

blue scilla flood   the slope   today
the house damp   feverish in the cold

the house red with a fever
brilliant yellow glow   all supplies

our red house you would say
has a high fever   & sunburn
the small indigo flowers cold
their single foot in the chilly earth
& windows just troublesome jackets.

afternoon drift

that ear to the floor rattling
whose heart like a child speaking
dance like a drummer   dreaming
lost   in Sunday

"Mythology tells us that where you stumble, that's where your treasure is."

—Joseph Campbell

I

Balmy skitterish night   now
2 a.m.   Insects singing, breezes
fluttering sweet hay & grasses in my
little attic window   a car door slams
at Carrie & Debbie's next door
calm & coolish airs sweep softly
outside I hear the airs pick up
& toss the trees
frogs & crickets & bugs of the night sing
Louder

II

last nights of summer
last balmy breezes of summer under the window

last balmy breezes through summer's window screen
moths gone   june bugs fled   mosquitoes removed
from the evening

Mosquitoes removed from the evening   moths gone
June bugs fled lone cricket &

the 2nd cutting of hay   last balmy breezes
through summer's window screen

apples

from 10 Weeks with *The Times*

New York Times
Vol. CXLVIII

Can we do a poem on a page of *The Times*
A day in the life of a city
a picture of a woman on a balcony
people jump up and down upstairs
Is there listening without writing it down?
a gerbil in one of those little steel wheels talks back

all lines   end in e

the animosity precipitated by the
It was a day of autumn brilliance
testament to a primordial pastime
their rapturous loudest champions astride blue and white
phoric fans as they crept along a one
in a rollicking ticker-tape
The Yankees deserve this parade
and more
They gave New York the best season that we will ever see
however technical or tentative the
actual arrangements they had made
nine days and nights of tortuous necrophilia
visible, seemed to underscore
for the next several hours at the
Each side blamed the other for the
the East Room of the White House
rial map, but the reconfiguring of the

to do things that were
yahu arrived in Wye a man whose
visible, seemed to underscore the
intelligence officials by surprise
will have a state
that would bring to 40 percent the

it was the weight of those tiaras
it was the other and that absence   melting
songs that are quiet in ambush

New York Times
Vol. CXLCIII

The Halloween Parade in Greenwich Village

The verdigris eye will turn to mold
Investors will plant marigold and tulip
keep an eye out for the wives of the politicians spouting
numbers
                    Digital confusion
                    on the Chrysler Building's drum set
Their blank Faces like a small basket-full of perfect hard melons
with hair to go   on the side
the apples depart zinc zinc   soon to be everywhere
limes
the thin chic dime
Saturdays bend long dinosaur necks encircling the stars
sharing the flora
the wind
this newspaper
tepidly tepidly
the magnificent
sheer, pasty   when you were putting one foot
into the soup   and rowing several paddles out to those
standing

It's beige
it's like champagne
it's called bamboo
The hacker's mantra "information wants to
be free"   & behind closed doors
the Vatican is conducting the 1st inquisition of the Inquisition
The truths that modern Americans seem to hold self-evident   are
mostly those that indulge the self
but now someone says "California
has a big pile of Republican moderates . . . "
pitch cold dark with sharp bright stars
There's John Glenn   having breakfast in
that diner in the sky   "god Speed!"

"It's only words . . ."
—BeeGees

the carcass of the metal sculpture of a horse   twisted agony
a few feet away fires burn   jellybean windows glow
suddenly a choir blurts out   explodes

A speaker swivels chest high in newsprint Is that a
leather jacket a brown leather jacket hollow reeds glow from the side of his
head   he wears no hat   he has not hat on   he is speaking   to someone
else   someone below the edge of the photo   no one is looking at anyone
but the microphones   the microphones are paying attention
they pick up every snort   they have hoop dreams

New York Times
Vol. CXLVIII

Nina from Miracle Mist
Looking for Mary . . .

Chrome & glass doors swing open
Jane   with the sun behind her

An example of the heart of birds
                          twilight polka dots

the object across from you
the rubber hose that eats its own tail

cigarette shifters make a deal with coyote

sunset the color of the watery syrup poured from a freshly opened can
of peaches   her face that launched a thousand suits
                            in the square admitting nothing

pitched battles in the streets
two scientists win Nobel for finding a way to value risky financial investment
                                        then   go bankrupt

fired
rubber bullets   tear gas   and water cannons at thousands
freeze frame students in beachcombers dash   for cover

odd quiet
from gates
in a storm

Ann, the world is big with beauty
a tumbling darkness full of lights
the crashing roll of steel on steel   of
trains   spreading   into the night

Or

She comes in after midnight
she eats the last of the pasta
she does the dishes
What a deal!
No leftovers

Forgive me   Excuse me
I drank the rest of the champagne
it was still bubbly
            (I had to light a candle in
            the darkened kitchen)
it went right to my head
I hadn't had lunch or dinner

jets of gas & dust shoot from all sides of the
comet's nucleus as it rotates a quarter turn

& in the darkened kitchen
I had to light a candle   to
the virgin in her prime
by now she was to me like
a suspect in a mystery

catching atoms

from the solar wind   a treasured smidgen of the sun

                              but

never mind
the champagne was cold
& full of tiny spheres

a huge flag fills the town green   as big as any tree

the band plays all the America pieces

the book sale at the library just finishing   Folding tents   packing

up books not sold   small crowd   some in chairs   some standing about

gorgeous fall Sunday afternoon   But

    no leaves have gone magenta   or even coral streaked

or that popping yellow we all fancy   just a thick green humming in the branches

a terrible lushness of verdigris   a sound that mocks the sound that running water makes

in the desert that sounds like people talking   a murmurous cistern ruckus that flees

"I got sick of all that purity: want to tell stories." —Philip Guston, 1970

tracks

the most intensely
romantic sight
on earth
the impoverished
little towns of upstate NY
fiercely stormed by snow

abandoned

"the one with the
  most numbers wins"

My soul and I went on
a strange journey

crazy houses
a frozen snowy
landscape

the long blunt
whistle & smoke
of the engine
blown back

along our view
from the train

the woman who
has made neediness
an art form

I'm not looking
for purity—the
world's not pure

little cars could be seen
speeding along the
frozen highway

fusillade: 1. shots fired simultaneously or in rapid succession.
something that gives the effect. 2. an outburst of criticism

to be broke in

to be brok en

Commuter train in an endless row of grey New England winter days

the train advanced through snowy landscape of forest and marsh as if in some European novel
the passengers returning from a day of work hushed to silence by the gathering darkness & the snow
that hung in big bunches from everything standing outside   even the boisterous and merrymaking
conductors had fallen silent, immersed in their books   so that a pall of melancholy settled over the
inner compartments   wherein   we fled forward   a long vestibule of gloom over the shuddering rails

from an Edinboro notebook

for Regina Geib

Turn here   this must be Edinboro

the porches and long lawns   are pale in this blurry mist

I actually haven't seen what birds soak up the sky

Or   restless forms that gather and relax the view

it's empty as a cake of soap   perched on a shower ledge

O Wet   now beaded torrents thud&roll the parking lot

small bursts of forest soar straight up   & sudden where the

houses stop   small farms pump at open gaps of   new stubble

otherwise it's goldenrod & chicory   red clover & that flea-like daisy

lots of opportunity for striding   or singing to the cornfields

to be itinerant   squawking so   & drenched with tofu days

pristine as unused chalk   I thought I'd take that walk to visualize

what I could be by bushy ditches overrun with clumps of orange & ochre

O Water tower   marking where the town begins   & Knight's video store

Hound's Head Inn

At night I snap off kitchen
lights   &
look through glass doors across the deck
over the railing   past a thicket of criss-
crossing winter branches   across
a thin highway   to a building illuminated
by a tall yard lamp that throws   a glittering
stark yellowish pinky light on a greyish white
facade beside a sombre   red t'orange likewise
blue sign with a Hound's Head
or
on the other side of which I stare into
Setting for a Fairy Tale by one Joe
Cornell exactly stark winter white &
glittered yellowish pink from a   yardlamp
brittle stork-etched winter branches through
whose spaces Cornell's *Untitled (Rose Castle)*
glitters in soft yellow winter light of yardlamp
completely still in one dimensional facade
between us goes 6N West & cars pop stunned
& shining every now &then
but mostly silence   as the gleaming Hound's Head Inn
its lighted   flat front & sign   a velvet darkness
holds it in a frame.

Crossroads Dinor

Curtains disguise the moon   & lend
to inky dark a glaze of white
"Monet never painted cars by his bridges" & so
these that could but never smoke   assemble
at table   nearest logs aburst
seal of a soon-to-be believed angel flying past
us   as we have supped   & toasted by that blaze
blond&beige students bring the menus   & the plates flat
on the corner   the only hill's a mural   this was trolley
103   rang Edinboro   to & fro's main street
if you were here to dine with us   the frosted spirits
in the historical picture books in the little library
in the basement of the police station
would fill your eyes and sneeze and cough as we do

In Edinboro

Here the cemetery has the best view of the lake
& striped & zigzagged families
in small cottages dabbled white & onyx   along the shore   wave
to boaters   sizzling in pastoral light   that seeps
across the water   in a rushing gold assault
as though a herd of elbows splashed   O
loco performance space!   toward me Professor temporar
disquieted by the gleam   Cold-hearted expose!
A woman draws collected rainwater
from a tub   pours a bucket
here   a bucket there   her
gardens & my crazy
rocking heart   She
swings   the bucket   as she goes

for Steph

"the place where the ducks walk on the fish"

is almost in Ohio but manages residence in PA
when you drove us there the day was dark & ripped
the shackish stall selling bread & tidbits to
feed the carp   was closed   it was late   it was
almost December   below the bridge
the lake poured into a curved drop   a miniature
Niagara   or thumbnail shaped & Carp   so many
they replaced the water   & the Mallards as   if they
floated treading   instead walked on the large &
rolling bodies that swam on each other's charcoal shape
mouths opened   the color of peonies

earth rained up

sky rained down

rain

no earth

no sky

for Ulysses   and Georgia O'Keeffe

From the window of Ulysses' room
a garage light has been
left on by someone for
someone who has yet to come home

a garage light left on
for someone by someone

In the blackness of night
a solid bar of light

COLOPHON

Erosion's Pull was designed at Coffee House Press in the historic warehouse district of downtown Minneapolis. The text is set in Kinesis.

FUNDER ACKNOWLEDGMENTS

Coffee House Press is an independent nonprofit literary publisher. Our books are made possible through the generous support of grants and gifts from many foundations, corporate giving programs, individuals, and through state and federal support. This book received special project support from an anonymous donor, and the Witter Bynner Foundation. Coffee House Press receives general operating support from the Minnesota State Arts Board, through an appropriation by the Minnesota State Legislature and from the National Endowment for the Arts, a federal agency. Coffee House receives major funding from the McKnight Foundation, and from Target. Coffee House also receives significant support from: the Buuck Family Foundation; the Bush Foundation; the Patrick and Aimee Butler Family Foundation; the Foundation for Contemporary Arts; Stephen and Isabel Keating; the Outagamie Foundation; the Pacific Foundation; the law firm of Schwegman, Lundberg, Woessner & Kluth, P.A.; the James R. Thorpe Foundation; the Archie D. and Bertha H. Walker Foundation; TLR/West; the Woessner Freeman Family Foundation; and many other generous individual donors.

This activity is made possible in part by a grant from the Minnesota State Arts Board, through an appropriation by the Minnesota State Legislature and a grant from the National Endowment for the Arts.

To you and our many readers across the country, we send our thanks for your continuing support.

Good books are brewing at coffeehousepress.org